TRUE CRIME

ORGANIZED CRIME

John Townsend

Chicago, Illinois

For information, address the publisher:
Raintree, 100 N. LaSalle, Suite 1200, Chicago, IL 60602

Customer Service: 888-363-4266
Visit our website at www.raintreelibrary.com

Printed and bound in China by South China Printing Company.
08 07 06 05 04
10 9 8 7 6 5 4 3 2 1

Library of Congress Cataloging-in-Publication Data
Townsend, John, 1955-
  Organized crime / John Townsend.
     p. cm. -- (True crime)
  Includes bibliographical references and index.
  ISBN 1-4109-1094-6 (library binding-hardcover) -- ISBN 1-4109-1172-1
(pbk.)
  1. Organized crime--Juvenile literature. I. Title. II. Series.

  HV6441.T68 2004
  364.1'06'0973--dc22

2004012878

Acknowledgments
Alamy pp. 42 (Ron Chaple), 27 (Tobias Hohenacker); Associated Press pp. 24–25, 40, 26 (Vincent Yu); Corbis pp. 6–7 (Alain Schein Photography), 8–9, 12–13, 40–41, 4–5, 5, 11, 19 (Bettmann), 22 (Diego Lezama Orezzoni), 33 (George H H Huey), 30–31 (Greg Smith), 15, 28 (Harcourt Index), 10–11, 16–17 (Hulton Deutsch), 5, 32 (Mona Reeder Dallas Morning News), 33 (Nathan Benn), 41 (Niall MacLeod), 6 (Peter Turnley), 35 (Reuters), 8, 25, 31 (Ric Ergonbright), 18 (Richard T Nowitz), 36–37 (Yves Forestier); Hulton Archive pp. 43 (American Stock/Archive Photos), 20 (Harry Todd); Hutchinson Library pp. 26–27 (Michael Macintyre); Interpol p. 37; Lonely Planet p. 24 (John Hay); PA Photos/EPA pp. 30, 19, 34; Peter Newark's American Pictures pp. 10, 12, 13; Photodisc/Harcourt Index p. 23; The Kobal Collection pp. 16, 21, 15, 38, 39; Tudor Photography p. 9.

Cover photograph of dollar bills reproduced with permission of Robert Harding Picture Library

Every effort has been made to contact copyright holders of any material reproduced in this book. Any omissions will be rectified in subsequent printings if notice is given to the publishers.

The paper used to print this book comes from sustainable resources.

CONTENTS

Any words appearing in the text in **bold** are explained in the glossary. You can also look out for them in the "Word Bank" at the bottom of each page.

LARGE SCALE

Organized crime covers all sorts of activities. From street gangs to large criminal organizations working across the world, they all use bullying and fear to get their way. They deal in:

- car theft;
- robbery;
- drug dealing;
- **smuggling** weapons, people, or works of art;
- gambling;
- **fraud,** blackmail, and bank crimes.

The bald man with a scar down his face looks up. He calmly strokes the white cat on his lap. His voice is soft. "Allow me to introduce myself. I am Ernst Blofeld. They told me you were killed in Hong Kong. You only live twice, Mr. Bond."

The scene is from the James Bond movie *You Only Live Twice.* Ernst Blofeld is the boss of Spectre, an organization with members who know one another only by code numbers. All the members are wanted by the police for their crimes in many countries around the world. Any who do not show trust in Blofeld are quickly **executed.**

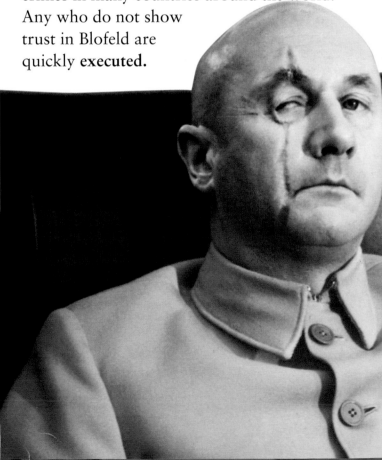

executed killed as a punishment
fiction made-up story from the imagination

THE REAL WORLD

In the movie, Spectre deals in stealing, kidnapping, and **blackmail** to make money. But Spectre does not really exist. Ian Fleming, the writer of the James Bond stories, made up the name. It is just **fiction.** The bad news is that there are organizations around today just like Spectre. They may not be run by men with white cats, but they do have violent members who will kill anyone who gets in their way. These groups want money and power. They will do anything to get both. This is the world of big-time **organized crime.**

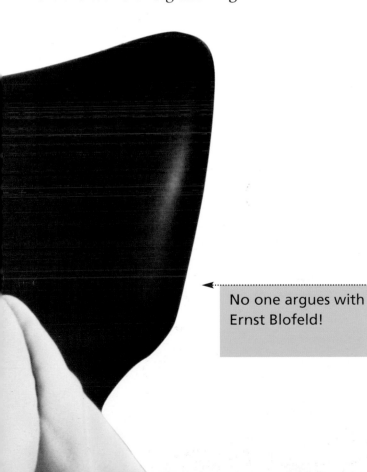

No one argues with Ernst Blofeld!

FIND OUT LATER . . .

Who were the gangsters of the past?

What are the mysteries of the Mafia?

What threats from organized crime face us today?

fraud   false or dishonest trick to get money

GANGSTERS

Organized crime involves people working together. It is run like a real business. Each person has a set job and an overall boss. These organizations are called gangs. They are **professional** operations.

A large garage, for example, might not be all it seems. It may sell top-of-the-line cars. But it may also be dealing in stolen goods and drugs—from the criminal **underworld.**

The real problem comes when one gang upsets another. If there are **rival** gangs in the same city, the bullets start to fly. That is when anyone can get hurt, and they often do.

YOUTH GANGS

In the 20th century, street youth gangs grew in Los Angeles and other cities in the United States. The Bloods and the Crips are well-known youth gangs of Los Angeles. Many of them have bad reputations for being involved in organized crime.

The police are always on the tail of gang members.

WORD BANK   loyalty   never letting anyone down and always showing commitment

DOWNTOWN

Many of the gangs at work today are part of multimillion-dollar organizations. They have taken years to grow into big businesses. But how did they all start?

Gangs of criminals joining together to make money are nothing new. The first cities had **bandit** gangs. Robbers worked together to protect each other. Many of them came from the poorer areas of town, where robbing and murder became a way of life. Joining a gang gave people protection and a sense of belonging. It also gave them the chance to get rich from more daring crimes.

PASSING THE TEST

To join a gang such as the Crips, people have to learn the rules and pass a test. This is called "the knowledge." They must swear **loyalty.** This may mean committing a crime or risking their lives. Then they perform a test of bravery. For example, the new **recruits** must walk along a line of gang members who beat and kick them. If they make it, they are in.

Stealing and selling cars is just one activity for organized criminals.

CHICAGO

Gangs of criminals were big trouble in some U.S. cities. At the end of the 1800s, people flooded into the United States from across the world. Most **immigrants** were honest and hard-working, but some were not. In the poorest areas, people turned to anger, greed, and violence.

Chicago became one of the centers of organized street crime. Many Italians came to the city to start businesses. If they had a visit from the Black Hand (*La Mano Nera*), it was bad news. The Black Hand was a gang that demanded money. People had to pay up to protect themselves. If not, an armed gang would come.

FROM BAD TO WORSE

Gangs got rich by running dishonest businesses. They demanded money and used threats. Their money-making projects were called **racketeering**. This name was used after some New York gangs held dinners to make money. These became known as rackets because of all the noise they made. Gambling, drinking, and **bribing** the police, lawyers, and politicians made matters worse.

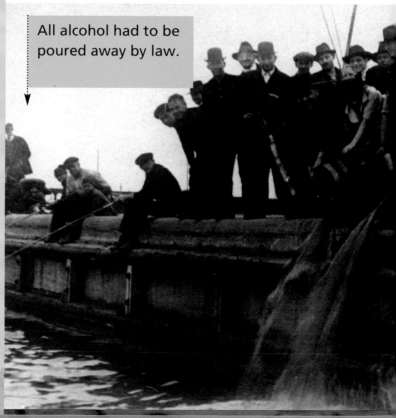

All alcohol had to be poured away by law.

WORD BANK

bootlegging   getting and selling illegal alcohol
immigrant   settler from another part of the world

GETTING A HOLD

At the start of 1915, the Black Hand gang set off 55 bombs in Chicago. They were trying to show who was boss. Some Italian-Americans set up the **rival** White Hand gang to fight back. The streets became dangerous. Rowdy gangs attracted drunken fights.

The U.S. government had to act. In 1920 it made a law banning the sale of alcohol. But this was just what the crime gangs needed. They began to make, sell, and **smuggle** beer and whisky. There was a lot of money to be made from this. As a result, Chicago now had some of the most ruthless American **gangsters** in history.

THE 1920s

The time when alcohol was **illegal** in the United States was called **prohibition.** It was against the law to make or sell alcoholic drinks such as whisky, gin, or beer. So that was just what criminals began to do. This was called **bootlegging,** after whisky smugglers from long ago who hid bottles in their long boots.

prohibition   when something is forbidden—such as making and selling alcohol

AL CAPONE

One of the most famous men in 1920s Chicago was Al Capone. As a teenager, Capone was part of the dreaded Five Points Gang of New York. In 1919 he joined another gang that controlled the south of Chicago. He was just twenty. A few years later he was a big-time gangland boss in Chicago.

Capone's career of terror lasted through the 1920s. Money, power, and murder made him public enemy number one. He made a fortune from **smuggling** alcohol. His **illegal** gambling bars were open day and night. He was soon making over $100,000 a week.

A CITY JUST RIGHT FOR CRIME

At the start of the 20th century, gangs in downtown Chicago (above) became so well organized that the police could not deal with them. They could not cope with so much crime. The police made many mistakes, and the criminals were soon running the city.

The horrors of gang crime on Valentine's Day 1929.

WORD BANK

illegal   against the law
massacre   killing of lots of people

MURDER

No one got an important job in Chicago unless Capone said so. Some people thought he was a hero. Other gangs hated his power. One gang leader, "Bugs" Moran, began to plot against him. Capone decided to act first.

On February 14, 1929, Capone sent his gang over. They dressed as policemen and gunned down six of Moran's men. Because February 14 is Valentine's Day, this became known as the Valentine's Day **Massacre.**

No one could prove that Capone was behind the killings. But a few years later he was caught for tax **fraud.** He was 32 and went to prison for seven years. This ended his power at last.

STILL FAMOUS

Al Capone (below) was let out of prison in 1939, at the age of 40. Just eight years later he died of a **stroke.** He was buried in Mount Olivet Cemetery in Chicago. Movies of his life of crime have kept his name alive around the world. The first movie based on his life was *Scarface* in 1932.

smuggle   secretly bringing goods or people into a country
stroke   sudden illness caused by a clot of blood in the brain

"BABY FACE" NELSON

"Baby Face" (above) was born in 1908 in Chicago. By the age of fourteen, he was a car thief. He was called Baby Face because he looked so young. He became a bank robber and joined the Dillinger gang in 1934. He shot many policemen and FBI agents. He was eventually killed in a gun battle.

Chicago's Biograph Theater, where Dillinger was shot.

GANG LIFE AND DEATH

Many violent people joined **bootlegger** gangs in the 1920s. One was George "Machine Gun" Kelly. His wife was also a bootlegger, but she wanted more. She got George a machine gun and made him practice shooting. He joined a bank-robbing gang as their machine-gunner and held up many banks.

It was George's wife's idea to kidnap a millionaire named Charles Urschel. They demanded a **ransom** of $200,000. They almost got away with it, but the ransom money was **traced** back to them.

Kelly was sent to jail in Alcatraz prison, the famous high-security prison built off the coast of San Francisco. He died there in 1954.

FBI   Federal Bureau of Investigation, which deals with serious crime in the United States

DILLINGER

John Dillinger was a name everyone feared. He was a robber and a murderer. In the early 1930s, Dillinger and his violent gang robbed banks and police stations in the United States. He broke out of prison three times, killing guards as he did so. The Dillinger gang killed yet another policeman in a Chicago bank robbery. The **FBI** set out to stop him once and for all.

One night in 1934, Dillinger took two friends to a movie theater in Chicago. One of them had warned the FBI, so they were waiting for him. Five shots were fired, and John Dillinger died in the street, aged just 31.

ORDINARY

"Johnnie's just an ordinary fellow. Of course, he goes out and holds up banks and things, but he's really just like any other fellow."

Mary Kinder, John Dillinger's girlfriend

GET·DILLINGER!
$15,000 Reward
═══ A PROCLAMATION ═══

WHEREAS, One John Dillinger stands charged officially with numerous felonies including murder in several states and his banditry and depredation stamp him as an outlaw, a fugitive from justice and a vicious menace to life and property;

NOW, THEREFORE, We, Paul McNutt, Governor of Indiana; George White, Governor of Ohio; F. B. Olson, Governor of Minnesota; William A. Comstock, Governor of Michigan; and Henry Horner, Governor of Illinois, do hereby proclaim and offer a reward of Five Thousand Dollars ($5,000.00) to be paid to the person or persons who apprehend and deliver the said John Dillinger into the custody of any sheriff of any of the above-mentioned states or his duly authorized agent.

THIS IS IN ADDITION TO THE $10,000.00 OFFERED BY THE FEDERAL GOVERNMENT FOR THE ARREST OF JOHN DILLINGER.

HERE IS HIS FINGERPRINT CLASSIFICATION and DESCRIPTION. ━ ━ ━ ━ FILE THIS FOR IDENTIFICATION PURPOSES.

John Dillinger. (w) age 30 yrs., 5-8½. 170½ lbs., gray eyes. med. chest, hair. med. comp., med. build. Dayton, O., P. D. No. 10587. O. S. E. No. 559-646.

F.P.C. (12)
```
        M  9  R  O  O
        S  14 U  OO 8
13  10  0  0  0
 u  R  w  w  w
 5  11  15 I  8
 u  U  u  w  u
```

FRONT VIEW

Be on the lookout for this desperado. He is heavily armed and usually is protected with bullet-proof vest. Take no unnecessary chances in getting this man. He is thoroughly prepared to shoot his way out of any situation.

GET HIM
DEAD
OR ALIVE

Notify any Sheriff or Chief of Police of Indiana, Ohio, Minnesota, Michigan, Illinois.

or THIS BUREAU

SIDE VIEW

ILLINOIS STATE BUREAU OF CRIMINAL IDENTIFICATION
T. P. Sullivan, Supt.

---

ransom   payment demanded for the release of a prisoner

THE MAFIA

THE GANG

The Mafia is an organized **international** body of criminals that began in Sicily. It is now widespread around the world, especially in Italy and the United States.

Criminal gangs were at work in Italy and on the nearby island of Sicily for centuries. By the 19th century, some of these gangs had joined up to form an organization called the Mafia. Joining the Mafia gave members pride, power, and protection. If anyone cheated them, they just asked a Mafia hit man—someone payed to kill people—to pay a visit. But no one would cheat on a member of his or her own gang, called a family.

Mafia members spread through all Italian cities. Some were wanted for murder, so many left Italy. They went to other countries where the Italian police could not arrest them. In the 1870s, many headed for the United States.

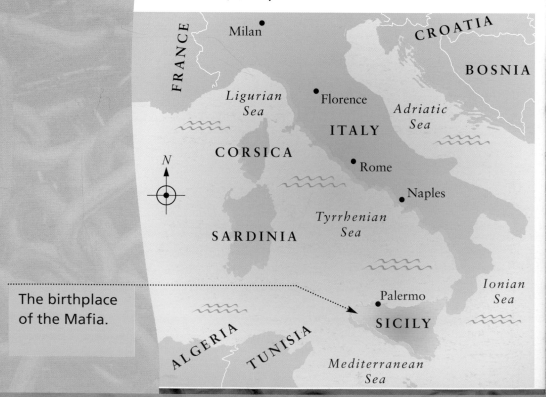

The birthplace of the Mafia.

WORD BANK   international   involves more than one country

THE MAFIA IN THE UNITED STATES

All big cities have their criminal gangs. In the early 1900s the big cities of the United States were just right for gangs such as these to **thrive**.

America was a new country that offered **immigrants** a new life. Most immigrants brought work, energy, and ideas. But a few brought other ideas—about crime. These ideas attracted more criminal immigrants. They teamed up to organize **illegal** gambling, drinking, and **racketeering**. In fact, they attracted the biggest **network** of criminals from Europe. Their name was already well known. The Mafia had arrived.

By the 1920s, the Mafia was running a network of organized criminal businesses in the United States. Its power began to spread across the whole country.

TODAY

Mafia gangs are still active in New York and New Orleans. In fact, Italian **organized crime** is big business around the world. Experts in Italy think this organized crime is worth over $100 billion each year. Although the Mafia does not have as much power as it used to, it may be behind a lot of this crime.

Goodfellas, a movie from 1990, was based on the true story of Henry Hill.

thrive   do very well

CRIME ON THE SCREEN

Many movies about **organized crime** have been set in New York. *Gangs of New York* (below) is about two **rival** gangs in the 1860s. In the movie, a gang called the Natives, led by the Butcher, is at war with the Dead Rabbits, an Irish **immigrant** gang.

NEW YORK

New York's earlier gangs included the Plug Uglies, the Dead Rabbits, and the Five-Points gang. They often got into fights. Irish and Italian gangs clashed all the time.

One of the most powerful Italian Mafia leaders was Nicholas Morello. In 1916 he went to make peace with his enemy, Pelligrino Morano. But Morano's men were waiting with machine guns. They shot Morello dead. Morano was shocked when the **bribes** he paid the New York police did not keep him out of prison. For him, crime did not pay after all.

LEONARDO DiCAPRIO   DANIEL DAY-LEWIS   CAMERON DIAZ

GANGS OF NEW YORK

AMERICA WAS BORN IN THE STREETS

contract   agreement, in this case an illegal agreement to kill a person for money

FAMILY MOBS

The next Mafia **godfather** to rule New York was Charlie Luciano. He joined other **mobsters** to make five families. They divided the city into five main Mafia gangs.

In 1929 Luciano was kidnapped and stabbed with an ice pick. He survived but still kept *omerta*—a **vow** never to reveal Mafia secrets, including the names of the people who had stabbed him!

By 1935 Luciano was known as the Boss of Bosses. He ruled with force, but ended up in prison. During World War II, he gave the U.S. Navy important information about Sicily. In return, the U.S. government let him return to Italy to live. Luciano died of a heart attack in 1962 while planning a movie of his life story.

MURDER INC.

The Mafia needed to hire killers to get rid of its enemies. A gang called Murder Inc. made it their business to murder people. Throughout the 1930s, Murder Inc. did many **contract** killings for gangs in New York. It was responsible for 500 to 700 murders around the United States.

As more Mafia members moved into town, crime became big business in New York.

mobster   Mafia boss of one of the gangs

vow   promise

LATER DAYS

John Gotti was born in 1940. He left school at sixteen to join the Gambino gang. This was one of the five Mafia families that controlled New York at the time. In the 1980s, Gotti became its boss.

Gotti dressed in expensive suits and pretended to be a salesman. He was really a ruthless **mobster.** The **FBI** knew this, but they did not have enough evidence to put him behind bars. In 1992 Gotti was at last sent to prison for life, for six murders and **racketeering.** He died in prison in 2002.

The FBI headquarters in Washington, D.C.

Cosa Nostra   criminal organization that grew out of Mafia gangs

RECENT TIMES

The "five families" of New York brought terror to the city for 70 years. President John F. Kennedy tried to control the Mafia's power in the 1960s. When he was **assassinated** in 1963, there were rumors that Mafia members were involved. These rumors have never been proven.

The Mafia's power in the United States today is nothing like it used to be. But it is still behind some drug and gun dealing, **fraud,** and **money laundering**. Money laundering is a big criminal business. The Mafia helps criminals to disguise stolen cash as legal savings. This stops the police from finding out where checks and bills come from. Money laundering also **invests** the Mafia bosses' **profits** to make sure they cannot be **traced.** They "stay clean."

Police seize goods **smuggled** by organized gangs.

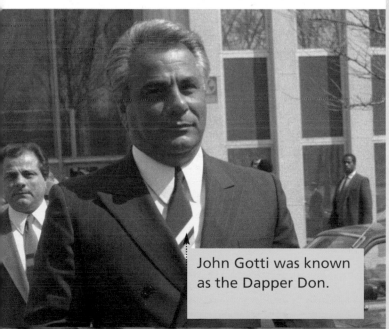

John Gotti was known as the Dapper Don.

STILL FIGHTING

"

Our mission is to reduce the threat to society posed by the American La **Cosa Nostra** (LCN) and Italian Organized Crime (IOC). Our goal is to get rid of these criminal organizations in the United States. To do this, we work to reduce their power and membership.

"

FBI Organized Crime Section

Criminal gangs are active all around the world.

UNITED KINGDOM

The docks and warehouses in the East End of London made rich pickings for thieves in the 1950s and 1960s. In addition to robbery, the gangs organized **protection rackets.** This meant people had to pay to avoid being attacked. Gang fights were common. Each gang tried to get more power than its **rival.**

The Kray brothers are one of the most famous British criminal families of the last 50 years. Reggie and Ronnie Kray were twins who started out as youth gang leaders in the 1950s. After **deserting** the British army, they became gangland bosses in London's tough East End.

CAN YOU BELIEVE IT?

Nearly a thousand small organized crime groups work in the United Kingdom. Most are British-born gangs, although Colombian, Italian, Chinese, Russian, and Jamaican **gangsters** work in London, Manchester, Glasgow, and Belfast. The biggest business for all these gangs is drug **smuggling.**

East End docklands in the 1960s.

CRIME FACT

Fifty-two murders in the U.K. in 1999 were probably linked to organized crime.

WORD BANK deserting   running away from being in the army; this is illegal

MAFIA LINKS IN THE UNITED KINGDOM

The Krays were quick with their fists. Both were bullies who demanded payment to leave people alone. With their older brother, the Kray twins ruled pubs and gambling houses. No one upset the Firm, as they were called.

In the early 1960s the Firm made contact with the U.S. Mafia to set up business deals in London. Ronnie became very violent and ruled through fear. An ex-gang member upset him, so the Krays killed him. In 1969 the twins were sentenced to 35 years in prison for this murder. The three Kray brothers are now dead. Their family empire of **organized crime** is over.

FINAL CHAPTER

Reggie Kray was the last of the big-time London East End gangsters. His death in prison in 2000 finally ended their story. Ten years earlier, a movie called *The Krays* earned him a lot of money. But he could not spend much of it from inside his prison cell!

From the movie *The Krays*.

protection racket   demanding money to "protect" someone from being hurt by criminals

RUSSIA

The Russian Mafiya has been organizing crime in Russia for years. It organizes **fraud, forgery,** and **smuggling** people. One group, called the Red Mafiya, deals in stolen art and antiques. Many Russian treasures have been smuggled to other countries.

FISHY BUSINESS

Caviar smuggling is a crime that is **unique** to Russian gangs. Caviar is an expensive food made from the eggs of sturgeon fish. Seventy-five percent of the world's caviar comes from Russian sturgeon caught in the River Volga and the Caspian Sea. **Poaching** and smuggling by organized gangs has made sturgeon very rare.

DID YOU KNOW?

Over a hundred large criminal organizations are at work in Russia. Russia's Department for Fighting Organized Crime thinks there are another 5,000 smaller criminal groups, which practice **money laundering** and drug smuggling.

Many of Russia's criminal gangs are based in the capital city of Moscow.

extinct   died out; never to return
forgery   making false documents, money, or paintings

Once poachers pull a sturgeon onto their boat, they cut it open to scoop out its eggs. They pack them into cans and throw the dead fish back overboard. This Caviar Mafiya has fast transportation links to get their **illegal** caviar out of the country. By **bribing** police at **checkpoints,** they can get across borders and escape.

THE LAW

The legal caviar business is now at great risk because sturgeon fish are becoming **extinct.** The giant beluga is the largest and most highly prized type of sturgeon. It has almost disappeared. That means people will pay even more for illegal caviar. Sturgeon fishing is now against the law.

BIG MONEY

Russia's legal sales of sturgeon dropped from 11,000 tons in 1992 to 550 tons in 2002. In parts of Europe and the United States, a few tiny spoonfuls of Russian caviar (above) sell for over $100. The shortage puts the price up even higher. No wonder organized gangs make big money.

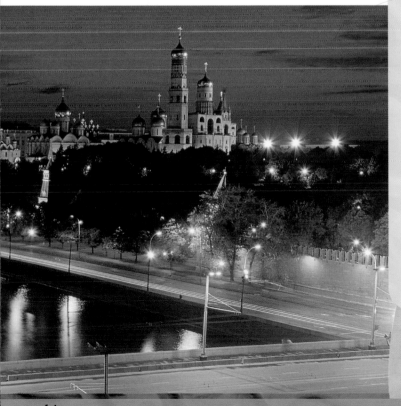

poaching   stealing animals by fishing or hunting illegally
unique   nothing else like it

23

ASIA

China, Japan, Hong Kong, and Taiwan have their own criminal gangs similar to Mafia "families." One of the names used for these is Tongs. These go back hundreds of years. Today, much of their crime involves making, stealing, and **smuggling heroin.**

Tongs also smuggle people. If anyone wants to get into another country to live, the Tongs can arrange it—for a price. They organize a lot of **illegal immigration,** charging huge fees to smuggle families out of Asia to the United States. The people are often packed like sheep into boats. The Tongs do not care, as long as they get their money.

HONG KONG

The Sun Yee On is the name of a large criminal organization in Hong Kong (above). It has about 56,000 members. Its gangs control crime in the streets. One of their interests is expensive cars. Thousands of cars have gone missing from Hong Kong's streets. Stolen cars can be sold for a lot of money.

Philadelphia's Chinatown.

WORD BANK   economy   anything related to money and finances

SLAVE LABOR

Once families get to the United States, they hope for a better life. But the Tongs still run their lives. Many illegal **immigrants** end up in **slave labor.** The Tongs are thought to run many clothes factories in Philadelphia, within a few miles of the city's Chinatown area.

Even if immigrants manage to set up their own businesses, Tong gangs will demand protection money. That means a weekly payment to the gang. Otherwise the Tongs burn down the business or attack the owner. The Tongs rule by fear.

BIG PROBLEM

The Chinese police believe there may be as many as 150,000 criminal gangs in Hong Kong and Taiwan (below). They are tied up with much of the business that goes on. This must cause a lot of harm to the **economy** in this part of Asia.

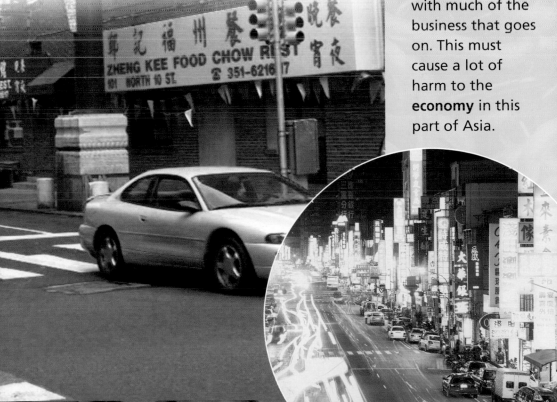

slave labor   being made to work hard for long hours with little pay

CHINA AND JAPAN

Many Chinese criminal gangs belong to an organization called the Triad. They work around the world, mainly in the Chinese districts of big cities. They run everything from drug and cigarette **smuggling** to gambling. But many of the gangs are best known for violence. Wars between Triad gangs have ended in murder.

March 2001

"Triad" schoolboys caught in Hong Kong

Eleven schoolboys have been arrested in Hong Kong. They were helping a triad crime gang to sell drugs and **pirate copies** of videos. Triads have been using boys as young as twelve or thirteen years old in some of their businesses. Fourteen adults were also arrested in raids.

Actors protest against Triads in the Hong Kong movie industry.

disobey   break the rules
offender   someone who breaks a rule

YAKUZA

In 1992 Japan banned all Yakuza criminal gangs. These gangs go back almost 300 years. In the 1950s, there were over 5,000 gangs across Japan. Today there are fewer.

Many Yakuza wear sunglasses and have slicked down hair. Some are missing fingers. Fingers are cut off if gang rules are broken! The first time a member **disobeys,** the top joint of the little finger is cut off. The freshly chopped fingertip is wrapped in a cloth and handed to the **offender's** boss. Next time, the whole finger is chopped off. A bad member may soon have no fingers at all!

MEN ONLY

The Yakuza do not trust women. They believe that women cannot fight like men. If there is a fight, a member must be ready to fight to the death, rather than lose the battle. Yakuza members must be willing to die for their boss. Their leader is called an *oyaban.*

Yakuza members cover their bodies with tattoos.

The samurai sword is ideal for a fight to the death—or for chopping off fingers!

AUSTRALIA

In the early 1900s, many Mafia members left Italy. They settled not only in the United States, but also in Australia. Some learned how to make fast money. They went to **remote** farms and made threats of violence unless the farmers paid protection money.

DUNGEONS

The dungeons of the Court of Victoria in Australia were used from 1884 to the 1950s. They were opened to the public in 2003. Les "Squizzy" Taylor was once locked up there. He was an Australian **organized crime** boss of the 1920s. He ran a gang until he was killed in a gunfight in 1927.

cannabis   dried leaves of the hemp plant; smoked or chewed as a drug, such as marijuana

After World War II, the Mafia spread into the cities. They grew **cannabis** and began to trade it for **heroin.** Some joined up with Triad gangs to develop a heroin business. The main port into Australia is Sydney (left), where Chinese and Hong Kong Triads now sell heroin. They can charge ten times what they pay for it in Thailand. They get rich quick from this very dangerous business.

Recent newspapers have told of the drugs threat from organized criminals.

GANGS INVADE AUSTRALIA

Eastern European gangs are a frightening new force in Australia's **underworld.** The ruthless **gangsters** are behind Melbourne's heroin trade. Some have links to the Russian Mafiya. To make bigger **profits,** the gangs add powder to the heroin to make it go further. This means the drugs they sell on the street can be **lethal.**

Russian gangs came to Australia in the 1990s. Some organize theft. Others **forge** passports for **illegal immigrants.** They tend to be violent, too. When these criminals say "I'm going to kill you," they mean it.

NEW ZEALAND

Triads and other organized criminal gangs have also settled in New Zealand. Some of the 14K Triad and the San Yee On arrived in the 1970s. Most major heroin raids in New Zealand have involved these criminal gangs. Attacks on the police are rare in New Zealand. This may change if organized crime keeps growing.

gangster   member of a criminal gang
remote   far away from towns and cities

The **United Nations** reports that there are more than 50 million regular users of heroin, cocaine, and other drugs around the world. The trade in illegal drugs could be worth as much as $400 billion a year. Organized gangs are behind most of the drug production.

Thousands of people around the world are part of the **illegal** drug business. They might grow the plants, make the drugs, **smuggle** them, or buy and sell them. They are all part of this huge **network** of **organized crime.** The business makes the bosses very rich. It makes other people very poor and very sick.

Columbia in South America is one of the well-known areas for growing and making cocaine. This drug is made from the cocoa plant. Groups of people who make the drugs and sell them are called **cartels.** Colombian drug cartels are large organized gangs. They provide 80 percent of the world's cocaine.

Police seize cocaine in Peru.

WORD BANK   cartel   organized group that controls the making and selling of a product

DRUG SMUGGLING

The bosses of the drug gangs are often called drug **barons.** They find all sorts of ways to smuggle drugs into different countries. The U.S. police once learned that a Colombian drug cartel planned to buy a submarine. What better way to avoid getting caught than to smuggle drugs under water?

Other drug smugglers use animals. When crates of snakes have been searched on ships, strange things have been found. Balloons filled with **heroin** have been found inside boa constrictors! Smugglers once hid heroin in the cages of deadly snakes. The security guards were meant to be too scared to search the cage. The plan did not work.

HEROIN

Heroin is made from the opium poppy (below). But this multimillion-dollar business does not use the latest high-speed transportation. Much of Europe's heroin starts off on camels! These animals carry the drugs through Afghanistan into Eastern Europe. The heroin is then smuggled on into markets in the United Kingdom, Holland, and Germany.

Drug smuggling can end in trouble!

United Nations   world organization of countries formed in 1945 to promote peace and security

PEOPLE-SMUGGLING

Human **migration** is nothing new. For centuries, people have left their homes to find a better life in another country. Today more and more people from poor countries try to move to Western Europe, Australia, and North America. Criminal gangs are always there to help—for money.

The criminals promise to take **migrants** to a better life. But they do not tell them the full story. Often the migrants are crushed into small trucks or boats. **Hygiene** on the boats is poor. What little food and water they have soon runs out. The journey can be total misery, or even **fatal.**

A CRUEL TRADE

People-smuggling has become a way of making big money for criminal gangs. It involves moving large numbers of people around the world. Stricter immigration laws today and careful checks at borders make migration difficult. **Illegal** migrants turn to organized people-smugglers for help. Often they wish they hadn't.

Illegal immigrants were crushed to death in this truck.

endangered species   animals in danger of becoming extinct

ANIMAL SMUGGLING

Criminal gangs use the same routes that they use for drugs, guns, and people to **smuggle** wild animals. Many of the animals die on the journey. Gangs such as the Russian Mafiya smuggle **endangered species** to sell as pets. Smuggled birds from Australia have even been swapped for **heroin** in Thailand.

TERROR

The crew and guards on the boats can be violent. Sick people are often thrown overboard. In stormy seas, the crowded boats are at great risk.

Getting to shore can be dangerous, too. It may mean steering the boat along a rocky coast in the dark. The migrants have to scramble or swim to shore without getting caught by the police. Because they are now **illegal immigrants,** they must obey the gang who brought them in. This often means working for the gang for many years to pay off the huge cost of the journey. If not, their family back home must pay up or face torture. Or even death.

migration   traveling long distances to find a new home
migrant   someone who travels to a new country to live

MISSING ART: REWARD $972,000

An oil painting by the famous painter Pablo Picasso was stolen from a yacht in 1999. The ship *Coral Island* was docked in the French port of Antibes. An organized gang of thieves stole a work of art called *Dora Maar* (above), which is worth $7.3 million. So far, there is no news of the painting.

ART SMUGGLING

Many paintings, works of pottery, and pieces of jewelry are worth a fortune. But if thieves try to break into a house, a museum, or a gallery to steal one of the treasures, they have a problem. They must sell the art to get their money. They will get caught when dealers know the work is stolen.

Organized crime gangs work with a **network** of criminal dealers. They will **smuggle** the art out of the country quickly. They might demand **ransom** money for the art to be returned. Or they may find a buyer who does not mind if the art is stolen. Either way, art theft can make organized criminals rich.

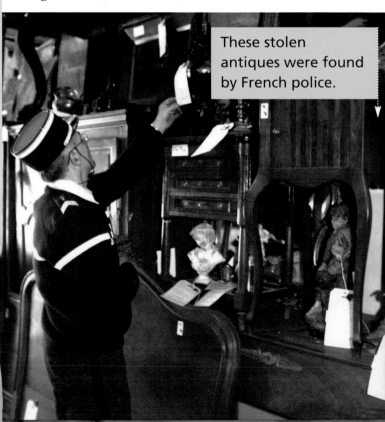

These stolen antiques were found by French police.

corrupt   willing to be dishonest when offerred a favor or reward

NEWS FROM 2003

Nine paintings from the art collection of Russia's famous artist, Sergei Bugayev, have been stolen. They disappeared from Bugayev's home outside St. Petersburg. The missing works are valued at $250,000.

When Bugayev discovered the theft, he called the local police. When they arrived, the police refused to take any action. They said there was no **evidence** of a break-in.

So why didn't the police believe Bugayev? Many people think that the Russian Mafiya **bribe** the police to ignore their crimes. Organized crime **thrives** if the local police are **corrupt.** Once the criminals pay the police, they can even get away with murder.

MISSING ART: REWARD $1.8 MILLION

In 2003 thieves stole a painting from Drumlanrig Castle in Scotland (below). The picture was by the famous artist Leonardo da Vinci. It was called *Madonna with Yarnwinder*.

The police found the getaway car abandoned not far from the castle. But the theft is still a mystery. The painting is worth up to $55 million. Where is it?

Police at Drumlanrig Castle investigate the missing painting *Madonna with Yarnwinder.*

evidence   proof or information from the scene of a crime

FIGHTING BACK

The misery, terror, and cost from **organized crime** affect all countries. Air travel and the **Internet** have made organized crime a **global** problem of the 21st century. It is very easy to do deals and travel all over the world. Small gangs of bullies can now join a huge **network.** But the police forces around the world can also join up. When criminals travel from country to country, an **international** police force is watching. It is called **Interpol.**

Interpol was set up for tracking down organized crime that operates around the world. Today, it is the biggest police organization. There are 181 member countries over five continents. Interpol never sleeps!

PROGRESS

" Our world has seen big changes in the last twenty years. Organized criminals have been quick to take advantage of these changes to satisfy their greed for power. "

The **FBI**

Interpol   international police force that works across many countries

INTERPOL

Interpol allows police forces to work together. They can quickly share information about criminal gangs on the move. Much of its work involves finding out about gangs and tracking where they are. Their crimes are usually related to **trafficking** of weapons, drugs, and human beings. The other big crimes are **money laundering, cyber crime,** and terrorism.

Interpol works around the clock. It receives, stores, and sends information to all its member countries. Sometimes this will be in the form of "wanted" posters. Details of criminals and their gangs can flash around the world in seconds. Now there is no corner where criminals can hide from the law.

INTERPOL

Have you seen this person?

PFAHLS, LUDWIG HOLGER
Born: 12/13/1942
Nationality: German
Age today:
61 years old

The German authorities are offering a reward of $9,000 for information that leads to the capture of Dr. PFAHLS.

Interpol headquarters in Lyon, France.

A lot of stories are told about the Mafia. People imagine men in long coats, hats, and dark glasses waiting in the shadows. Under their arms they carry a violin case. The case holds a machine gun. This is just one of the **myths** about how Mafia members look.

DO NOT BELIEVE IT!

Wild stories warn you to beware in Moscow. They say the Russian Mafiya watch every street, ready to kidnap any visitor. Tires squeal as a black car with darkened windows whisks away yet another victim.
Kidnappings do happen, but most tourists are safe.

James Cagney in the 1938 film *Angels with Dirty Faces*.

myth   made-up tale, told over the years and passed on

Marlon Brando in *The Godfather* (1972), another movie about the mafia.

THE WRONG IDEA

From the world of James Bond to television series such as *The Sopranos*, **organized crime** makes good entertainment. Old **gangster** films of the 1940s also gave audiences false ideas about criminal gangs. Books, movies, and television help to keep many of the myths going. They can also make criminals seem exciting. Or they can give the wrong idea that all **immigrants** from Italy, Russia, or China belong to dangerous gangs.

Another myth is that the Mafia makes big money from sports. Some say they place their bets and then fix the events. Fixing means they force or **bribe** the athletes or referees to make sure one side loses. This hardly ever happens!

IN THE NEWS

Newspapers report **organized crime** all the time. Some of the biggest stories happen when gang leaders go to prison.

Hard Times for the Mafia

New York, 2003

New York's five Mafia family bosses are all behind bars for the first time.

Joseph Massino was the last to be jailed. He was said to be the boss of the Bonanno crime family.

Peter Gotti was the head of the Gambino crime family. Now he is in prison, too. He follows a family **tradition** of getting locked up. Since the 1990s, the Gambino gang has appeared in more books and television programs than any other Mafia family.

THE JAILING OF JOSEPH MASSINO

❝ There was a time when no mob boss was even **convicted.** This is one more step in the fight against the mob. ❞

Ronald Goldstock, former head of the New York Organized Crime Task Force, 2003

John Gotti (on the right) in court before he was sent to prison.

WORD BANK   convicted   found guilty and punished

BACK IN THE NEWS

Roberto Calvi was the head of an Italian bank. He also had links with members of the Mafia in Sicily. In 1982 he lost a lot of the bank's money. He went on the run to London, using a false passport. Two days later he was found dead, hanging from Blackfriars Bridge. It was a mystery. The police thought he must have killed himself because of all his worries. His family said it must have been murder. In 2003, twenty-one years later, more **evidence** came to light. Tests suggested that Roberto Calvi was murdered by the Mafia. Maybe they wanted to stop him from telling their secrets.

MAFIA LINK?

A study into Roberto Calvi's death took four years. It showed that he was killed in a construction yard. His killers then took his body by boat to Blackfriars Bridge (below), where they hanged him. In 2003 Calvi's son said a trial would one day convict his father's killers.

WHERE NEXT?

TIMES CHANGE

The Mafia is the biggest single **shareholder** in the American **economy** . . . They have more influence on the daily lives of all Americans than the government or Wall Street or even the Church. They can **manipulate** anything.

Joe Coffey,
Commander in
Chief of Detectives
Organized Crime
Homicide Task
Force, New York
Police Department,
1978

Organized crime is here to stay. Ever since the first gang met to organize a hold-up, the world has had to deal with criminals working together. Their methods have become more **professional,** with no thought for the people they harm. So how will organized crime change in the next ten years?

Smuggling of people, drugs, and weapons will always happen. But other organized criminals are likely to become threats to the security of countries. If gangs get hold of nuclear or chemical weapons, they would be able to make all sorts of demands.

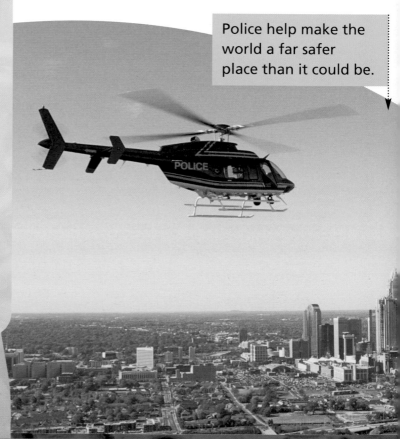

Police help make the world a far safer place than it could be.

WORD BANK

majority   greater part or percentage
manipulate   make something work to your own advantage

KEEPING ONE STEP AHEAD

By 2015 experts think criminal groups will be far more involved in **cyber crime**. They could **disrupt** government, police, and bank computers. **Interpol** is already keeping a close eye on this.

Criminals might get bigger, bolder, and more organized. But so will Interpol. Police and governments will continue to protect the **majority** of people. It is the majority, after all, who are honest, keeping the world far safer.

NEW TIMES, OLD PROBLEMS . . .

Crime changes and adjusts to different times. Professional gangs will always try to get rich at the expense of others. Some people argue that banning alcohol, drugs, and gambling will make the world safer. Others say that this will just let criminals run more **illegal** businesses and make huge **profits**. There will never be easy answers in the fight to stop organized crime.

Banning alcohol in the 1920s led to even more crime.

shareholder   owns part of a company

If you want to find out more about the criminal **underworld,** take a look at these books:

Blashfield, Jean F, *Interpol*. Milwaukee: Gareth Stevens, 2003.

McIntosh, Neil. *Just the Facts: Cyber Crime*. Chicago: Heinemann, 2003.

Wolff, Lisa. *Gangs*. Farmington Hills, MI: Gale, 2000.

DID YOU KNOW?

In Australia it is a crime in some states to:
- own a mattress without a mattress license;
- wear pink short-shorts after midday on Sundays;
- change a lightbulb unless you are an electrician!

THE FORTY THIEVES

Madame St. Clair, known as Queenie, ran a gang in New York in the 1920s. She called it the Forty Thieves. The gang was so tough that all the other **mobsters** left her and her turf alone!

CRIMINAL RECORDS

- The world's first speeding ticket was issued in the United Kingdom in 1896 to a man named Walter Arnold. He was traveling at 8 mph (13 km/h) in a 2 mph (3.25 km/h) zone.

- The most successful sniffer dog was a Labrador from the United States named Snag. He found 118 different hoards of hidden drugs worth an amazing $1 billion!

- The oldest person to be hanged was 82-year-old Allan Mair in 1843 in the U.K. He was hanged sitting down, since he was unable to stand.

- The world's largest safe-deposit-box robbery took place in 1976. A group of highly trained criminals stole more than $39 million worth of goods from a bank in the Middle East.

COSA NOSTRA

The name **Cosa Nostra** means "our thing." It started hundreds of years ago in Sicily to protect ordinary local people from the police and from **bandits.**

45

GLOSSARY

assassinate   to kill a leader

bandit   robber or murderer; member of a gang

baron   powerful business person

blackmail   threats to make someone pay

bootlegging   getting and selling illegal alcohol

bribing   paying someone powerful to act illegally in your favor

cannabis   dried leaves of the hemp plant; smoked or chewed as a drug, such as marijuana

cartel   organized group that controls the making and selling of a product

caviar   expensive food made from the eggs of sturgeon fish

checkpoint   border where guards inspect papers, cars, etc.

contract   agreement, in this case an illegal agreement to kill a person for money

convicted   found guilty and punished

corrupt   willing to be dishonest when offered a favor or reward

Cosa Nostra   crime organization that grew out of Mafia gangs

cyber crime   crime involving computers and the Internet

deserting   running away from being in the army. This is illegal.

disobey   break the rules

disrupt   interrupt or break up

economy   anything related to money and finances

endangered species   animals in danger of becoming extinct

evidence   proof or information from the scene of a crime

executed   killed as a punishment

extinct   died out; never to return

fatal   end in death

FBI   Federal Bureau of Investigation, which deals with serious crime in the United States

fiction   made-up story from the imagination

forgery   making false documents, money, or paintings

fraud   false or dishonest trick to get money

gangster   member of a criminal gang

global   around the whole world

godfather   name for the head of a Mafia "family"

heroin   highly addictive drug made from the opium poppy

hygiene   standards of health and cleanliness

illegal   against the law

illegal immigration   arriving in another country without permission

immigrant   settler in a new country from another part of the world

international   involves more than one country

Internet   worldwide network that links all computer networks together

Interpol international police force that works across many countries

invest put money into shares, business plans, or savings accounts

lethal dangerous and deadly

loyalty never letting anyone down and always showing commitment

majority greater part or percentage

manipulate make something work to your own advantage

massacre killing of lots of people

migrant someone who travels to a new country to live

migration traveling long distances to find a new home

mobster Mafia boss of one of the gangs

money laundering turning stolen money into legal savings or shares in businesses

myth made-up tale, told over the years and passed on

network web of connected groups that work together

offender someone who breaks a rule

organized crime large organizations involved in crimes in many countries

pirate copy CD, DVD, or video that has been copied illegally

poaching stealing animals by fishing or hunting illegally

professional showing commitment and skill in a full-time occupation

profit money made by selling something for more than the price originally paid for it

prohibition when something is forbidden—such as making and selling alcohol

protection racket demanding money to "protect" someone from being hurt by criminals

racketeering running a dishonest and illegal business

ransom payment demanded for the release of a prisoner

recruit new member

remote far away from towns and cities

rival person or team competing against another person or team

shareholder owns part of a company

slave labor being made to work hard for long hours with little pay

smuggle secretly bringing goods or people into or out of a country

stroke sudden illness caused by a clot of blood in the brain

thrive do very well

trace track down

tradition custom or event that happens over many years

trafficking movement between countries

underworld part of society that lives by organized crime

unique nothing else like it

United Nations world organization of countries formed in 1945 to promote peace and security

vow promise

INDEX